In Switzerland

written by **Judy Zocchi** illustrated by **Neale Brodie**

dingles&company New Jersey

For Diane Yasargil

First printing

PUBLISHED BY dingles&company
P.O. Box 508 • Sea Girt, New Jersey • 08750
WEBSITE: www.dingles.com • E-MAIL: info@dingles.com

Library of Congress Catalog Card No.: 2004094737
ISBN: 1-59646-006-7

Printed in the United States of America

ART DIRECTION & DESIGN BY Barbie Lambert
ENGLISH EDITED BY Andrea Curley
RESEARCH AND ADDITIONAL COPY WRITTEN BY Robert Neal Kanner
EDUCATIONAL CONSULTANT Bridget Riley Turnbach
ART ASSISTANTS Erin Collity & Sara Sagliano
PRE-PRESS BY Pixel Graphics

Global Adventures

The Global Adventures series takes children on an around-the-world exploration of a variety of fascinating countries. The series examines each country's history and physical features as well as its most popular customs, activities, and foods.

Judy Zocchi

is the author of the Global Adventures, Holiday Happenings, Click & Squeak's Computer Basics, and Paulie and Sasha series. She is a writer and lyricist who holds a bachelor's degree in fine arts/theater from Mount Saint Mary's College and a master's degree in educational theater from New York University. She lives in Manasquan, New Jersey, with her husband, David.

Neale Brodie

is a freelance illustrator who lives in Brighton, England, with his wife and young daughter. He is a self-taught artist, having received no formal education in illustration.. As well as illustrating a number of children's books, he has worked as an animator in the computer games industry.

In Switzerland **GERMAN** is what most people speak.

German is spoken in most of Switzerland. However, the country has four official languages: German, French, Italian, and Romansh.

This is my best friend, Anna.
I'm pleased to meet you.

SWISS BANKS are famous around the world.

Banks are an important part of the Swiss economy. The Swiss have very strict rules about who can get information about a person's bank account.

BANK

The SWISS FRANC is what people spend.

The Swiss franc is the name of the currency of Switzerland. One hundred rappen make up one Swiss franc.

CHOCOLATE
1 Fr.
HELVETIA

An ALPENHORN is long and curled.

An alpenhorn is a curved wooden horn. It can be from 3 to 12 feet long. It is used by herders to call their cattle.

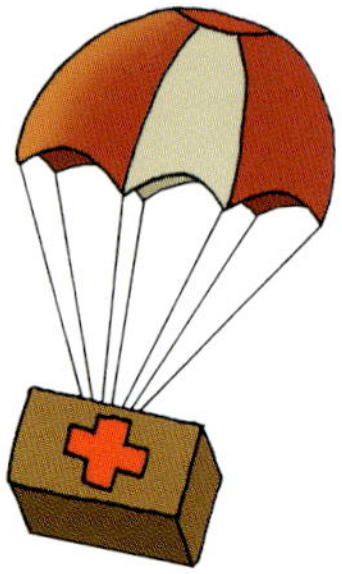

In Switzerland the RED CROSS was established.

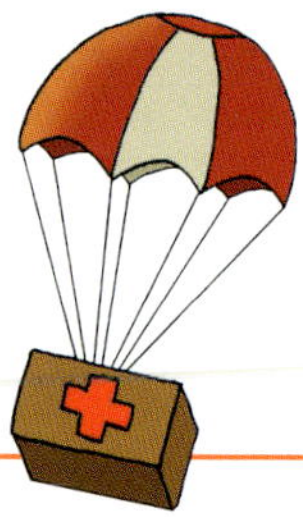

A red cross is the symbol of the Red Cross. This organization protects and helps people during wars and natural disasters. It is not connected to any country.

The **ALPS** are where skiers go.

The Alps is a large mountain range that stretches across Europe. It goes from Austria in the east to Slovenia, Italy, Switzerland, Liechtenstein, and Germany in the west.

It's a crime to pick EDELWEISS.

Edelweiss is a flower that grows high in the Swiss Alps. People are not allowed to pick these flowers. This helps keep the species from disappearing.

ST. BERNARDS rescue people in the snow.

The St. Bernard is a very large, intelligent, and gentle dog with a thick coat. It was bred to rescue people in the snow.

In Switzerland **FONDUE** is a favorite dish.

Cheese fondue is made with a melted cheese mixture. Bread cubes are dipped into the mixture and eaten.

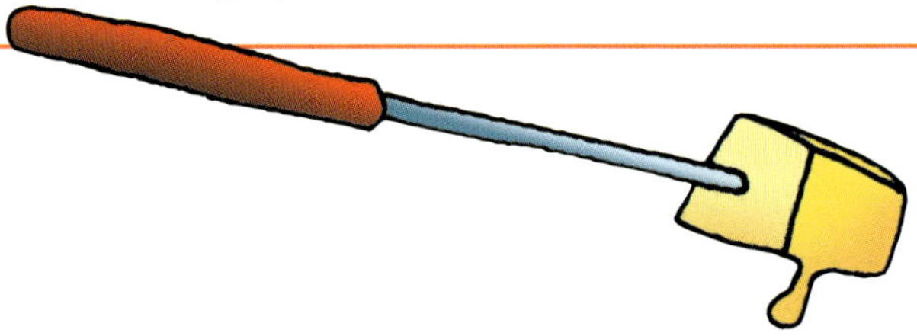

WATCHMAKING
is a popular trade.

Watchmaking is an important part of the Swiss economy. The Swiss make about half of all the watches in the world.

BOBSLED racing was born.

Bobsleds were first raced down icy passes in the Swiss Alps.

The first batch of MILK CHOCOLATE was made.

In the late 1800s, two Swiss men experimented with chocolate. They combined condensed milk with cocoa powder and created milk chocolate.

SWISS culture is fun to learn.

GERMAN

SWISS BANKS

SWISS FRANC

ALPENHORN
(al-pen-HORN)

RED CROSS

ALPS

EDELWEISS
(AY-del-vis)

ST. BERNARDS

FONDUE
(fon-DOO)

WATCHMAKING

BOBSLED

MILK CHOCOLATE

Lucerne: Near this city is Glacier Garden, where a giant glacial pothole containing fossilized shells and palms was discovered. This proves that 20 million years ago the area was a tropical palm beach–before glaciers covered it.

Zurich: Spend a day getting lost walking down the narrow alleyways of this old town. If you count the fountains, you'll reach more than 1,000!

See what you can discover at every turn!

Zermatt: This famous skiing resort town is at the foot of the Matterhorn. It's a village without cars–only horse-drawn sleighs and carriages are allowed.

OFFICIAL NAME:
Swiss Confederation

CAPITAL CITY:
Berne

CURRENCY:
Swiss franc

MAJOR LANGUAGES:
German, French, Italian

BORDERS:
France, Germany, Austria, Italy, Liechtenstein

CONTINENT:
Europe

ABOUT SWITZERLAND

Long ago the land that is now Switzerland was inhabited by the Helveti Celts. It was later conquered by the Romans. In 1648 Switzerland became independent. In 1798 France conquered the country, but in 1815 Switzerland's independence was reestablished. Switzerland adopted a constitution--the set of laws of the country--in 1848. There are 26 cantons, or states, in Switzerland. The Swiss Alps run across the south-central part of Switzerland. Most of the people live in the northern part of the country because it is less mountainous and has a more temperate climate. Switzerland has not taken part in any world war. The Swiss are famous for their banks, watches, cheeses, and chocolate.

UNDERSTANDING AND CELEBRATING CULTURAL DIFFERENCES

- What do you have in common with children from Switzerland?
- What things do you do differently from the children in Switzerland?
- What is your favorite new thing you learned about Switzerland?
- What unique thing about your culture would you like to share?

TRAVELING THROUGH SWITZERLAND

- To which neighboring country is the capital, Berne, closest?
- In which section of Switzerland are the Swiss Alps located?
- On what continent is Switzerland located?

TRY SOMETHING NEW...

Have a fondue party! Melt some cheese and chocolate. (Ask an adult for help.) Dip bread cubes into the cheese mixture and fruit into the chocolate. Don't forget to tell your friends all you have learned about Switzerland.